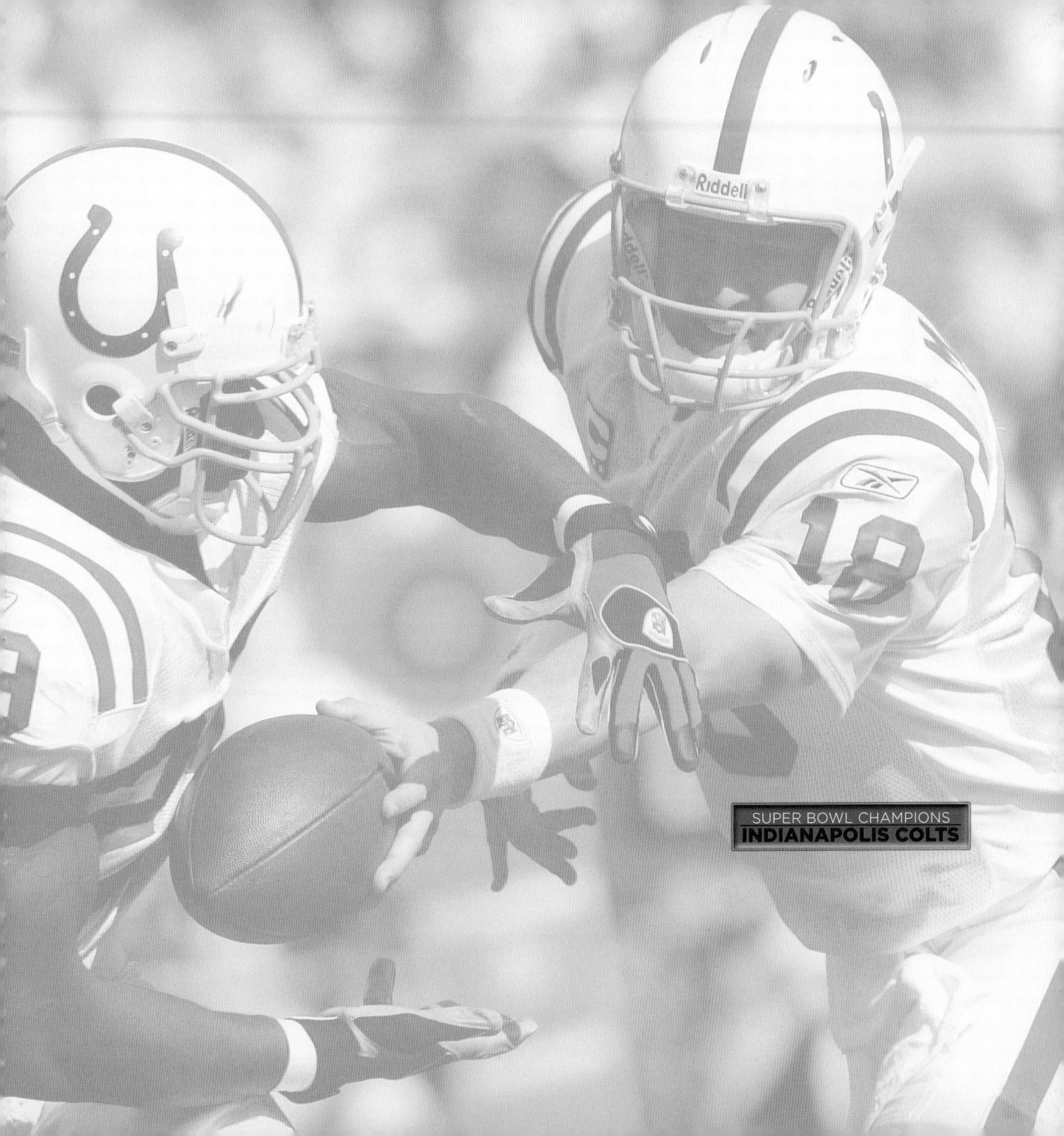

SUPER BOWL CHAMPIONS
INDIANAPOLIS COLTS

RUNNING BACK
DONALD BROWN

SUPER BOWL CHAMPIONS
INDIANAPOLIS COLTS

AARON FRISCH

CREATIVE EDUCATION

Published by Creative Education
P.O. Box 227, Mankato, Minnesota 56002
Creative Education is an imprint of The Creative Company
www.thecreativecompany.us

Design and production by Blue Design
Art direction by Rita Marshall
Printed in the United States of America

Photographs by Corbis (Richard Cummins), Getty Images
(Diamond Images, Focus on Sport, George Gojkovich,
Chris Graythen, Otto Greule Jr., Jeff Gross, Andy Lyons,
Donald Miralle, Darryl Norenberg/NFL, Sam Riche/MCT,
Frank Rippon/NFL, Joe Robbins, Marc Serota, John
Sleezer/Kansas City Star/MCT, Rick Stewart/Allsport, Rob
Tringali/SportsChrome)

Library of Congress Cataloging-in-Publication Data
Frisch, Aaron.
Indianapolis Colts / Aaron Frisch.
p. cm. — (Super bowl champions)
Includes index.
Summary: An elementary look at the Indianapolis Colts
professional football team, including its formation in
Baltimore in 1953, most memorable players, Super Bowl
championships, and stars of today.
ISBN 978-1-60818-377-7
1. Indianapolis Colts (Football team)—History—Juvenile
literature. 2. Baltimore Colts (Football team)—History—
Juvenile literature. I. Title.

GV956.I53F75 2014
796.332'640977252—dc23   2013010566

First Edition
9 8 7 6 5 4 3 2 1

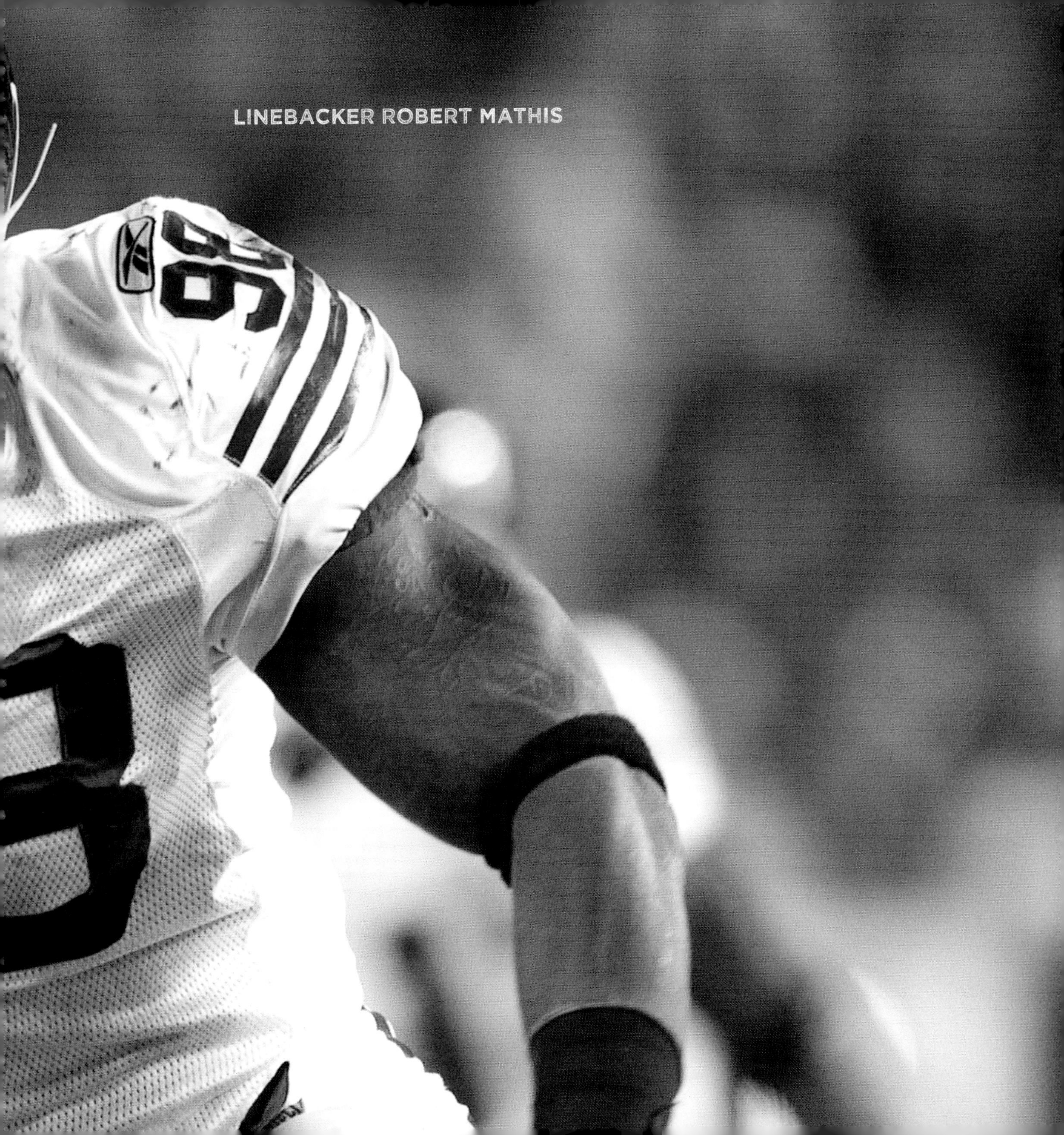

LINEBACKER ROBERT MATHIS

GINO MARCHETTI / 1953–66

Gino was a strong defensive end who liked to **sack** quarterbacks. He never seemed to get tired.

TABLE OF CONTENTS

JOHN MACKEY / 1963-71

John was a tight end who caught many passes. Even though he was big, he was a fast runner.

THE HORSESHOE TEAM

In 1953, a football team was formed in Baltimore, Maryland. Horse racing is popular in Maryland, and a young male horse is called a colt. The Colts football team was born!

BERT JONES / 1973-81

Bert was a tough quarterback.
He played even when he was
hurt and could throw the ball far.

WELCOME TO INDIANAPOLIS

Indianapolis, Indiana, is a city near the middle of America. Indianapolis sports fans like car racing and basketball. But they love to watch Colts football, too.

DEFENSIVE END DWIGHT FREENEY

A FAMOUS MOVE

The Colts were popular in Baltimore. They won three world championships. In 1983, the Colts moved to Indianapolis. It was a sad day in Baltimore but a happy one in Indianapolis.

"I think I'm proudest of making my parents proud."
— ERIC DICKERSON

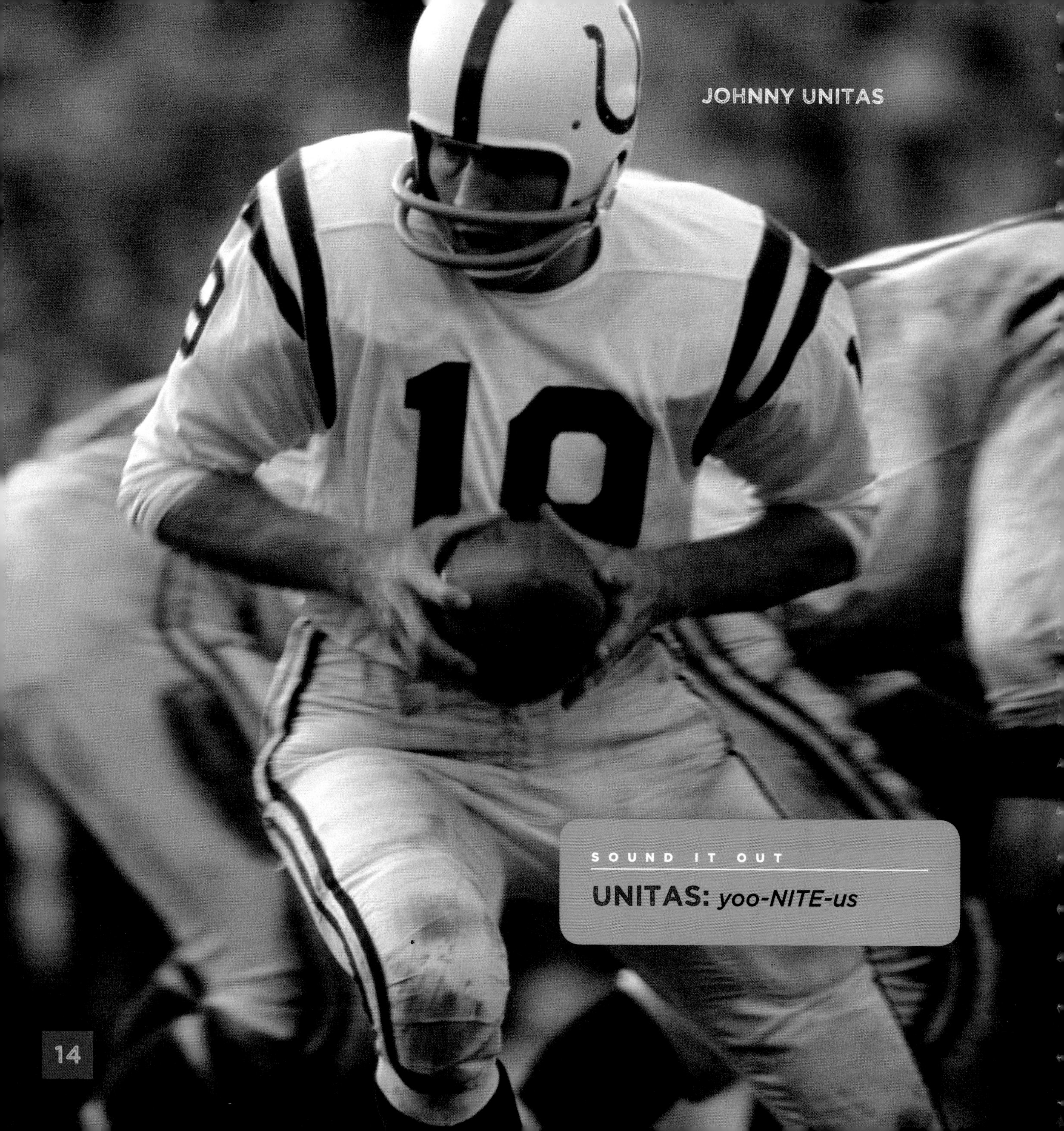

SOUND IT OUT

UNITAS: *yoo-NITE-us*

THE COLTS' STORY

When the Colts were still in Baltimore, they had a tough quarterback named Johnny Unitas. He helped the Colts win the National Football League (NFL) championship in 1958 and 1959.

FAMOUS COLTS

TONY DUNGY /
2002–08
Tony was a smart and calm coach who helped the Colts become NFL champions after the 2006 season.

BOB SANDERS / 2004-10

Bob was a star safety for Indianapolis. He was short (only 5-foot-8), but he was a great tackler.

EDGERRIN: *ED-ger-in*

After the 1968 season, the Colts lost Super Bowl III (3) to the New York Jets. It was a famous **upset**. But two years later, the Colts won Super Bowl V (5).

After the Colts moved to Indianapolis, fast running back Eric Dickerson scored many touchdowns. But the Colts did not get to the **playoffs** very often.

EDGERRIN JAMES / 1999–2005
Edgerrin was a tough running back who took handoffs from Peyton Manning. Fans called him "Edge."

"Pressure is something you feel when you don't know what the heck you're doing."
—PEYTON MANNING

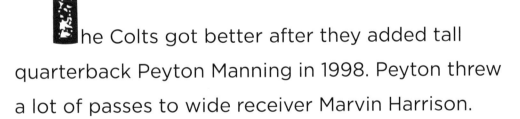

MARVIN HARRISON

The Colts got better after they added tall quarterback Peyton Manning in 1998. Peyton threw a lot of passes to wide receiver Marvin Harrison.

After the 2006 season, the Colts got to the Super Bowl. They beat the Chicago Bears 29–17 to win their first championship for Indianapolis!

SAFETY ANTOINE BETHEA

By 2013, Andrew Luck had replaced Peyton as quarterback. Fans were getting used to a lot of new players, but the Colts believed they could race to another Super Bowl soon!

ANDREW LUCK

21

CORNERBACK DARIUS BUTLER

FACTS FILE

CONFERENCE/DIVISION:
American Football
Conference, South
Division

TEAM COLORS:
Blue and white

HOME STADIUM:
Lucas Oil Stadium

SUPER BOWL VICTORIES:
V, January 17, 1971 / 16–13
  over Dallas Cowboys
XLI, February 4, 2007 /
  29–17 over Chicago Bears

NFL WEBSITE FOR KIDS:
http://nflrush.com

GLOSSARY

playoffs — games that the best teams play after a season to see who the champion will be

sack — tackle a quarterback who is trying to throw a pass

upset — a game in which the team that most people think will win ends up losing

INDEX